George's Mistake

By

Catherine Richardson

Dedication

To George,Noah and Milly. You have been the inspiration since day one.

Acknowledgement

Dad, I wouldn't be who I am without you. Unfortunately Dementia has stolen you from us. I wish you could have been present to see this and be proud.

About the Author

Kate Richardson born in Ipswich Suffolk, now resides in Oxford and works as a Biomedical Scientist for the NHS

George the worm lived in the ground

A wormhole was his home

He would very rarely leave it

As he could'nt see where he was goin'

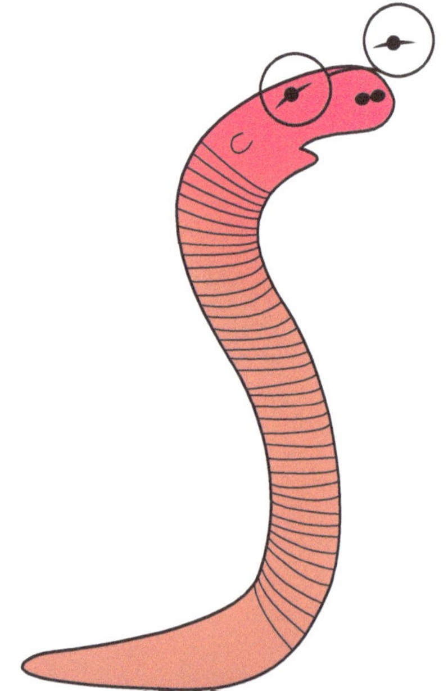

The birds swooped down and scared him so

He was sure he'd be their lunch

So he stayed in alone at nights

And practiced his punch

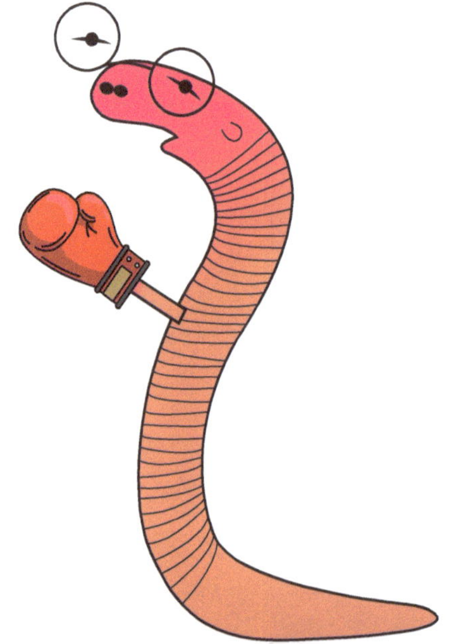

The day arrived when George did feel

More confident and strong

He ventured out to wiggle about

But not for very long

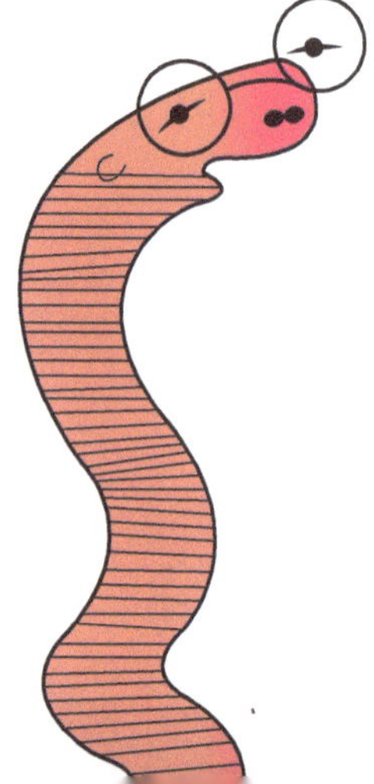

It wasn't long before the worm was

Snoring as loud as ever

Cosy and warm on his grassy chair

Sleep induced by the clement weather

Z Z Z Z Z

The snores George made were so very loud

It scared the local fauna

It woke the owls and sleeping moles

Who thought it might be thunder

One bird flew down to snatch up the worm

And eat him with his pecker

But luckily a mole popped up and

Saved him which was better.

z z z z z

The mole pulled George into his mound

They exchanged some idle chatter

But then the mole turned around

And ate George for his supper

So when you are all soft and pink

And others think your supper

Don't fall asleep in the open air

Or you'll end up fried in batter.

www.ingramcontent.com/pod-product-compliance
Lightning Source LLC
Chambersburg PA
CBHW042145030726
47599CB00002B/630